COMMONPLACES

FOR ADORNO, SONTAG, MADONNA, FUGAZI, TWOMBLY, PAVLOVA, ET AL

☼

COMMONPLACES

FOR ADORNO, SONTAG, MADONNA, FUGAZI, TWOMBLY, PAVLOVA, ET AL

JOSH RUSSELL

NEW MICHIGAN PRESS
TUCSON, ARIZONA

NEW MICHIGAN PRESS
DEPT OF ENGLISH, P. O. BOX 210067
UNIVERSITY OF ARIZONA
TUCSON, AZ 85721-0067

<http://newmichiganpress.com>

Orders and queries to <nmp@thediagram.com>.

ISBN 978-1-971740-00-3. FIRST PRINTING.

Design by Ander Monson.

Cover image by the author.

CONTENTS

FOR THEODOR ADORNO

Rare is the teenage son who thinks his father's Frankfurt School sociology books are cool. I listened to my dad's LPs when I was a little kid, but at fourteen, fifteen, sixteen no way I was dropping the needle on Chuck Berry or John Lee Hooker. Instead: cassettes of ABC and Madness and Big Country and Run DMC and the soundtrack to *Beat Street*. There was also no way I was going to read about how some tedious philosopher hated saxophones when I had Vonnegut and a fat omnibus of 1930s boys' aviation adventure stories my mom bought me at a library sale. In 1933 the Nazis revoked Adorno's right to teach, and he went into exile—England, New York, Los Angeles—until 1949, when he returned to Frankfurt. In the summer of 1969, while Adorno stood at the front of a Goethe University hall, trying to lecture on dialectical thinking, a student wrote on the chalkboard *If Adorno is left in peace, capitalism will never cease,* and three of that student's female classmates came to the lectern, bared their breasts, and tossed flower petals onto the old professor who'd called some of their friends *stormtroopers in jeans.* He died before the fall term began. I was one year old that summer. My dad spent a dozen years teaching sociology in Bloomington, Normal, and Highland Heights before he left academia. No student ever took off her shirt or threw petals at him or blamed him for capitalism's continuation—I asked. In *Minima Moralia* Adorno writes *In the end, glorification of splendid underdogs is nothing other than glorification of the splendid system that makes them so.* Here's the thing: It's underdogs all the way down.

FOR DEXYS MIDNIGHT RUNNERS

One day after school, on a sidewalk in Northern Kentucky, three hicks beat me up. Earlier, in the lunchroom, a cheerleader named Dawn asked me to smell a jar of Noxzema. When I bent to sniff, she shoved it in my face. Noxzema went up my nose and into my eyes. Unbeknownst to her and to me, the vice principal was watching, and he pulled us into his office. He lectured her while she cried and apologized and I repeatedly told him and her it was no big deal, I was fine. Almost immediately a rumor started that I'd gotten Dawn, the most popular girl in junior high, kicked off the cheer squad, and the sidewalk beatdown was based on that rumor—which wasn't true: the captain of the cheerleaders doesn't get in serious trouble for torturing a nobody. A week later I changed schools. Every morning for two and a half years thereafter I walked a mile of sidewalk along Alexandria Pike to a bus stop in an A&P parking lot and rode a public bus to a school in a different district. On weekends I made the same walk and rode the same bus past my new school and over the Ohio. I wandered Cincinnati sidewalks leading to Soul Train Fashions, which reeked of incense, to the optician on Fountain Square where I tried on Wayfarers I could not afford, to the record store where I bought cassettes—including Dexys Midnight Runners' *Too-Rye-Ay*.

MTV was added to my family's cable channels in late 1983, around my fifteenth birthday. I remember going to my new school and talking excitedly to my friends about our shared discovery. I didn't listen to the radio, so MTV was my introduction to pop music. The Buggles' "Video Killed the Radio Star," the first video shown on MTV, was still in regular rotation, along with others from the network's early days: "Brass in Pocket," "Rapture," "A Message to You Rudy." But what I remember most clearly is "Come on Eileen."

The video opens with historical context—what looks like newsreel footage of Johnny Ray, an American singer hugely popular in the early 1950s in the UK, greeting a crowd of adoring fans—context that frames a backstory shown in black and white snapshots—the narrator's parents, his mother holding what we assume is him as an infant, the narrator and Eileen as kids and then as childhood sweethearts—backstory that sets up a very 1980s present: young love, nagging boy who admits to a girl wearing nothing under her denim overalls that his thoughts about her *verge on dirty* (he wasn't the only one). In some scenes Eileen's friend pushes a toddler in a stroller along the sidewalk, the dangers of giving in to such nagging—but Eileen does appear finally to give in, and at video's end, she and the narrator walk off down the sidewalk into the night. The narrative was—and still is—exciting.

Of course I wanted to wear cool clothes like the people on MTV wore, do my hair like they did their hair, dance like they danced, suffer heartbreak and ecstasy like they did—*oh, Eileen*—but I've come to recognize the detail that most connected me to "Come On Eileen" was where the action took place. Like me, the people in the video walked and ran and danced and yearned on the sidewalk. Maybe if I'd been even a couple of years older the videos that would've hooked me would've been the ones that involved driving—"Ghost Town," "Life in a Northern Town"—but I didn't even have a learner's permit. I was an exurban flâneur. The sidewalk was my territory.

FOR SUSAN SONTAG

In *On Photography* Sontag writes *The shock of photographed atrocities wears off with repeated viewings, just as the surprise and bemusement felt the first time one sees a pornographic movie wear off after one sees a few more.* In the summer of 1984, I moved from suburban Cincinnati to suburban Washington, DC, and took a trip to New York to visit a friend who'd moved to Brooklyn around the same time I moved to Silver Spring. One day we set out to find a pornographic movie theater that would let us in. I was sixteen and he was fifteen. In Chinatown, we watched ten minutes of a subtitled flick in which the blurred crotches of the participants looked smeared. *It's itchy,* read the text at the bottom the screen, never a good thing to hear during a sex act. Frustrated, we headed for Times Square. The man in the ticket window blinked slowly when my friend told him we were eighteen. Once the place had been a picture palace. Its grand lobby was filthy. I remember being surprised the concession counter was abandoned, the candy case cracked and empty. Inside the theater, a dozen men sat far away from each other in a space that could've accommodated hundreds, shifting in squeaking seats and clearing their throats, dimly illuminated by glowing giants having sex. My friend and I sat silently and watched the frantic fucking. At one point there was a closeup of a huge penis—it must've been ten feet long—and suddenly a cat, black as a silhouette, ran across the stage and leaped onto the screen, drove its claws into the colossal cock, hung there for a few seconds, then dropped back onto the stage and ran off.

After a moment of stunned silence, everyone laughed.

In the same essay, Sontag tells us *All photographs are memento mori.* I'm trying to square that claim with her claim about pornography, and with the cat. Did the cat somehow remind me I must die? Did dirty movies limit my ability to be shocked, bemused, and surprised? Or did Betamax cassettes and that black cat distract me from death by repeatedly showing me a bemusing, shocking world? It's been so many years, that Times Square is gone, but the cat in my memory is forever running across the stage.

FOR ROBERT F. SIMON

When I pay $7.99 to download a 1966 driver's ed scare film I was shown in the summer of 1984—*The Third Killer,* produced by the Ohio State Highway Patrol and somehow starring Robert F. Simon, a character actor who played Willie Loman on Broadway, Darrin's dad on *Bewitched,* and a hundred-plus other stage, movie, and TV roles—I am reminded once again that fact-checking dulls nostalgia's pleasures. I want instead of a digital file, memory's montage: the stutter of the Super 8 projector, boys and girls sitting in the dark in driving simulators with the dashboards of circa 1977 Dodge Darts snickering at bad acting and goofy sanctimony while the pissed-off coach yells at us to take seriously a movie about a salesman named Rellik who eggs on men and women who look like our most uncool uncles and aunts to drive too fast and die in inevitable crashes, coughing to cover my laughter when coach asks, "What did you learn?" and the girl with the dark ponytail in my road skills group answers, "Don't become the kind of person who takes advice from someone whose name is *killer* spelled backward." When we turned right out of the high school's parking lot, what street was it onto? Was the next right the Jamaican driving instructor told us to take Wisconsin Avenue or Connecticut? When we followed it and then got onto the Beltway, did we see atop a hill the Mormon Temple and spray-painted across an overpass *SURRENDER DOROTHY?* Was it Wisconsin or Connecticut onto which we exited, then made another right, then another into the parking lot, where one of us got out of the back seat and switched with whoever was behind the wheel? I refuse to do the research. Nostalgia shuffles memory's under- and overexposed snapshots, a stack of prints from the one-hour photo processing place in the mall. A mixtape plays in the car stereo, Madonna and Run-DMC and Bad Brains. One of us brakes for a yellow and our instructor yells, "You could've made that light!"

FOR MADONNA

Over the toilet in the employees-only bathroom of the 7-Eleven was a poster that showed what different kinds of handguns, rifles, and shotguns looked like when they were pointed at your face. *REVOLVER* was at eye level when I peed. I was sixteen during the summer bookended by the introduction in late April of New Coke, and the publication in late August of nude photographs of Madonna in *Playboy* and *Penthouse*. "Like a Virgin" had fallen from number 1 to completely out of the top 40 by the time I started my summer job, but I still heard it all the time on the radio, along with "Material Girl," "Crazy for You," "Angel" (the most forgettable of Madonna's 1985 hits, which somehow reached number 5 at the end of June), and "Dress You Up," which broke into the Top 40 at the end of my time at 7-Eleven. Along with *Playboy* and *Penthouse* my 7-Eleven stocked *Penthouse Letters*, but I don't remember ever selling any of them. *Playboy* and *Penthouse* were vacuum-sealed like LPs, but *Penthouse Letters* wasn't, which is why I read it instead of the others: one Sunday morning I watched my manager, in front of the doughnut delivery dude, berate another employee for opening a *Playboy* during the 11-to-7 Saturday-to-Sunday shift. I'd never kissed a girl, let alone done any of the things described in *Penthouse Letters* in highfalutin or hardboiled prose even then I suspected was intentionally ridiculous. Madonna's love song is puritanical in comparison with what I read, which may have been why, though I wanted to hate it, I was secretly pleased when it came on after "Everybody

Wants to Rule the World" or "Things Can Only Get Better" or "Voices Carry": *Didn't know how lost I was / Until I found you.* The things happening in those letters were obviously fiction. What Madonna described seemed possible: … *your heartbeat / Next to mine.*

FOR FUGAZI

After much discussion in the last weeks of 1987, my girlfriend and I set about finding a place to lose what virginity we had left. History ruled out the car: a month or so before we got busted by the Park Police one night parked along Rock Creek below the glowing Mormon Temple. We ended up on dirty living room wall-to-wall in Wheaton when we went to feed a friend's family cat because he and his brother and his mom were out of town for Thanksgiving. A few days later I turned nineteen. In my memory of those days, we're always naked and trying and failing not to make noise while listening for a creaking stair or a slammed car door. In mid-December, we were walking near the National Gallery and its quiet rooms—so I'm wrong, my memory holds more than beds and couches and floors—when we came upon wheat-pasted broadsides that yelled *MESSE is a PIG*. A short manifesto below the foot-tall red block-letter *PIG* explained why he was. The posters, big and loud, seemed suddenly everywhere, and it felt like the revolution I'd naively wished for was afoot. Soon after my girlfriend and her family left for Christmas in Chile, from which they'd fled in the early '70s. It was safe now for them to visit, and they did every December, and I knew they were going, but the silence in their station wagon was still startling after I dropped them off at Dulles and drove back to their house in Silver Spring where I was staying while they were in Santiago. I let myself in with her father's keys. After a dinner of delivery pizza, I sat on the living room couch—where we'd made out many times—reading a book and feeling grown-up, when a timer clicked, the lamps turned off, and the quiet room went dark. A few days after Christmas my friend Al called to ask me if I wanted to go to a show at dc space. Maybe he knew I needed noise. Cover was $1.99 and the woman working the door made everyone take a penny when they gave her two singles. When I was next in line, she showed me the number on the tally counter: 125. I didn't understand. "Fire code," she explained. Behind me Al groaned. I asked if I could watch from the doorway. "You are tall," was her answer. I remember it was loud and somewhat sloppy and the volume and messiness soothed me. They closed with "Waiting Room." Twenty-one seconds in, the music abruptly stops for four seconds of silence. And then the song restarts. Almost four decades later, a lot of people know this; a YouTube video of an early live performance of "Waiting Room" has been viewed almost ten million times; those four seconds are no longer a surprise. But in December of 1987 Fugazi had yet to record even a demo, had yet to play out even a half dozen times, and when the music stopped, a woman screamed, as if frightened by the sudden quiet. I remember her scream, and I remember the heat of the crowd, and I remember the shock of cold and quiet when I stepped onto the street. People either whispered or yelled, senses skewed by transcendent noise.

FOR DJ SCOTT LAROCK & JASPER JOHNS

When DJ Scott LaRock samples Fat Albert asking *What can we get for sixty-three cents?* on BDP's "Illegal Business," he's paying homage to a TV show that in 1988 was a shared part of the just-completed childhoods of many of those of us listening to *By All Means Necessary*, and he's juxtaposing our knowledge of that innocent TV show against KRS-One's claims that *Cocaine business controls America / Ganja business controls America / KRS-One come to start some hysteria / Illegal business controls America.* (And now there's the additional juxtaposing of *Fat Albert*-era Cosby against rapist-era Cosby.) I came to contemporary art via Boogie Down Productions, Public Enemy, Run-DMC, Eric B. & Rakim. My high school girlfriend was a volunteer docent at the National Gallery, where I would go on weekend afternoons to meet her after her shift and she would lead me through exhibitions. It didn't take long before I started coming early to roam alone before I picked her up. It was during that roaming that I saw Jasper Johns, et al were doing something akin to what DJ Scott LaRock, et al were doing—mixing, remixing, layering, juxtaposing, heading Johns' advice to *Take an object / Do something to it / Do something else to it. [Repeat.]*—saw that *Flag* and "Illegal Business" are both *a very complex set of corrections.*

FOR HENRY JAMES

I was, at the age of twenty-three, one of the people on whom much is lost. At a graduate student conference in Baton Rouge, I met a woman who invited herself back to my garage apartment where we got only a single long kiss into an assignation before she apologized for changing her mind. We watched Letterman and drank coffee and made strange small talk and then I drove her to the home of the friend from her childhood with whom she was staying for the weekend. The next morning, she called and asked if I wanted to go to New Orleans with her and her friend to watch a Mardi Gras parade. Foolishly, I thought this was because she was having second thoughts about having second thoughts the night before. In the car, heading south along I-10, no one spoke. She told me she needed to study. Her friend was obviously sure I was there because something had happened the night before, something more significant than what had, in fact, happened. Alone in the back seat, I watched the woman I'd kissed underline in blue ballpoint a copy of *Daisy Miller* that'd already been heavily underlined in black, and soon I realized she was adding emphasis to every single line on every single page.

FOR ROLAND BARTHES

Quiet Riot's biggest hits were a decade old when they showed up in Baton Rouge at the live music venue where I worked as a doorman and bouncer. I knew the band and their songs from early-'80s MTV, back when they toured with Black Sabbath and played stadiums, rather than headlining Wednesday shows at small clubs in college towns. At load-in, I helped a roadie get a huge, battered Anvil wardrobe case off the bus and into the green room, where he proudly opened it to show me rows and rows of Polaroids of women's crotches neatly taped to the inside of the case's door. Each of the many dozens of snapshots had been framed so that the picture began just below the belly button and ended just above the knees. Beneath every woman was a motel bedspread. I wish I could say I was shocked by the groupies' nudity. In *Camera Lucida*, Roland Barthes explains to me that my blasé response is an example of *studium*, "a kind of general, enthusiastic commitment" to the subjects of certain categories of photographs (war, porn) that "derives from an average affect, almost from a certain training." I reply that the bedspreads are the *punctum*, the element that "will break (or punctuate) the *studium*," the element "which rises from the scene, shoots out of it like an arrow, and pierces me." I remind him that a "photograph's *punctum* is that accident which pricks me (but also bruises me, is poignant to me)." "Nothing more homogeneous than a pornographic photograph," he harumphs, quoting himself. I can quote too: "Mapplethorpe shifts his close-up of genitalia from the pornographic to the erotic by photographing the fabric of underwear at very close range: the photograph is no longer unary, since I am interested in the texture of the material." "You mean the bedspreads?" Barthes asks. "Yes," I answer, "and the fact that *every* Polaroid includes a bedspread. Repetition and reiteration both *studium* and *punctum*: 'sting, speck, cut, little hole—and also cast of the dice.'" Nudity that so amused the roadie I remember in the washed-out hues of an old Polaroid (probably because I want my long-delayed guilt over saying nothing, doing nothing, feeling almost nothing to fade similarly) while the patterned bedspreads are forever bright and weird.

FOR JOSEPH CORNELL & EDWARD HOPPER

In May of 1993, I went to The Art Institute of Chicago to see the Cornell boxes—*Soap Bubble Set, Dovecote, Untitled (Blue Sand Box), Untitled (Forgotten Game)*, etcetera—boxes I knew only from books and postcards but nevertheless loved, loved, loved, because I believed I shared with Cornell an aesthetic based on making monumental the jejune (moon cut from magazine, liqueur glass, yellow marble), making immortal the workaday (broken window glass, finches cut from who-knows-where, yellow rubber ball), and when I reached the end of a maze of galleries filled with statues of Shiva and Buddha, pointillist masterpieces, and many water lilies, the boxes thrilled me—alchemically they transformed culture's effluvia into timeless art!—but then I made the mistake of peeking over my shoulder: Behind me hung Edward Hopper's *Nighthawks*, a painting so lovely it transcends its ubiquity, and when I looked back at the blue glow of Cornell's *Untitled (Lighted Dancer)*, a blue glow that made the jejune and workaday dancer lovely by *not* making her monumental or immortal, merely illuminating her, I understood I'd misunderstood.

FOR GEORGE FRIDERIC HANDEL

At the end of our febrile first week together, Kathryn led me to the basement of Middleton Library. We were teaching each other who we were, what we liked, hoping each time we shared some secret, touched, turned away it would be okay to have told, tried, refused. She asked the music librarian for a Handel album, and we sat side-by-side, headphones plugged into a turntable, and listened to *Acis and Galatea.* Save bits and pieces of *Messiah* at Christmas, I'd not heard Handel before. Galatea sang to the birds in the pastoral landscape they needed to quiet down, because their *thrilling strains / Awake my pains, / And kindle fierce desire.* Then Acis's voice took over—*Where shall I seek the charming fair? / Direct the way, kind genius of the mountains! / Oh tell me, if you saw my dear! / Seeks she the grove, or bathes in crystal fountains?*—and Kathryn, grinning, began to cry. Fierce desire I'd shared with her. Holding her hand while she cried about Acis and Galatea detailing their love of one another, I shared something more.

FOR KATHRYN

Cleaning up one night after everyone else was asleep, I found under a library book on the kitchen counter the torn drawing. On one scrap, the crotch of a woman, triangle of scribbles, on another, the crotch of a man, disproportionately large penis hanging beside single ovaloid testicle. I pieced the picture together. The nudes stood side by side, nothing drawn below their thighs or above their innocent bellybuttons—or were they supine, perhaps postcoital? My daughter was at that time nine. What boy passed her this? She'd ripped it up but not thrown it away. I tried to remember how old I was when first I'd seen some kid's penciled version of sex, probably nine, maybe ten—and it hadn't been this chaste. I decided to talk to my daughter about the drawing in the morning. It would be a serious conversation. I went to bed feeling uneasy about entering, at age forty-six, a time in my life in which I would have to think about sex in a new way—and it occurred to me, just before I fell asleep, my disquiet was perhaps in part nostalgia for the moment in my childhood when, because of a dirty picture, a time in my life began in which I thought about sex in a new way. At the breakfast table I said, "I found a drawing of a woman and a man," and instead of looking embarrassed, my daughter looked amused, and my wife said, "I drew that. She wanted to know what a naked man looks like, so I drew that."

FOR JONATHAN SWIFT AND CLAUDE MONET

In "Resolutions 1699," Swift resolves *Not to tell the same Story over and over to the same People,* which is, in general, a good resolution. But what about Monet's *Les Meules à Giverny?* He painted twenty-five stacks of grain, each a slight variation: end of summer, foggy morning, sunset at thaw; haystack, wheatstack, grainstack. Six have snow on them and in their titles, but even their stories vary: morning, sunset, sunlight, overcast day. Painting and repainting, telling and retelling the same story to the same people, getting the light just right, the fog and the mist. Monet's dead, but his *meules* paintings are in museums in Chicago, Paris, Boston, Zurich, Minneapolis. So what if, Jonathan Swift, a tale told over and over outlives me in the museums of the minds of wife and daughter who roll their eyes when I tell the same story again and again and again, each iteration and reiteration and re-reiteration another wheatstack, grainstack, haystack?

FOR JEAN-MICHEL BASQUIAT

Jean-Michel Basquiat's eight-by-ten-foot *Untitled, 1982-1983* is composed of twenty-eight sheets of white paper torn from a spiral-bound sketchbook and mounted on a stretched canvas. Each sheet is covered in text: inscrutable flowcharts; crossed-out calculations; numbered lists; cryptic notes re the French Revolution, Hanna-Barbera cartoons, the Ottoman Empire, and historical and fictional figures (the Manchu Emperor, Hogarth, Admiral Rodney, Lex Luthor). This jumble of text and schemata draws focus away from the dominant image: in the upper middle of the artwork, a black face, maybe a mask, wears a broken version of Basquiat's signature three-pointed crown—an icon borrowed from graffiti taggers. To the left a black streak like a banner has written on it in white *SOP*—standard operating procedure?—and through the three letters there is a negating white line. I saw *Untitled, 1982-1983* at Atlanta's High Museum, in the first room of a three-gallery show of Basquiat's notebooks. In the second room was a silkscreened version of the same image, less than a quarter of the size of the original, and in negative—the original's blacks white, whites black. The mask and the text are suddenly reversed in how they capture attention: it's hard to look past the white face.

FOR GRANDMA RUTH

My grandmother died aged ninety-five. Before she passed, she wrote several dozen letters a week. She had a system to keep track of who was owed a letter—kids, grandkids, great-grandkids, far-flung relations—who she'd recently sent a letter, who'd responded. Grandma Ruth's hand was until the end steady and precise, albeit old-fashioned. Her graphomania meant I got news from Columbia, Missouri about what she was reading, what was in bloom, how many inches of snow had fallen. One of her last letters to me opened with this: *I did it again. I got all my writing supplies around me and fell asleep, well 1/2 asleep. I could feel my fingers writing words. I woke up and hadn't written a thing & sat there and did it again. So I got up and did a few walking chores and hope I can stay awake and write.*

FOR JORGE LUIS BORGES

Borges writes, *All men, in the vertiginous instant of coitus, are the same man. All men who speak a line of Shakespeare are William Shakespeare.* Shakespeare can cause pleasure I agree is akin to vertigo, as can coitus, as can one byproduct of coitus—my kid—who's diapers I changed when she was a baby, and whose hair I washed for a decade. Any squeamishness I ever had about my body disappeared when I was allowed access to the bodies of others. There was blood in my stool for a month so my doctor sent me for a colonoscopy and it turned out I had cancer. Six weeks later a surgeon used a robot to remove ten inches of my colon and a tumor from the body about which I had few complaints for forty-seven years. The topography of my asshole was altered. I did pelvic floor exercises to relearn how to hold my shit. Could be worse, could be dead. Instead, I got to walk my daughter to school in the morning and drive her to dance class in the afternoon and read to her at bedtime and laugh with her. I'm alive to speak lines of Shakespeare and Borges and to feel the bed and then the world fall away when my beloved presses my edited body down into twisted sheets.

FOR ELVIS

My oncologist told me he'd run a test to see if I had Lynch Syndrome, an inherited disorder that greatly increases the risk of colon and rectal cancer. Mainly this would be to see if my daughter was in danger. "Is it a blood test?" I asked. "We test the tumor," he explained. I was confused. The tumor was gone from me. "You have the tumor?" He nodded. "It's in the archive." I should've asked for details about the tumor archive. Instead, I imagined something like a vault in the hospital's basement.

After World War II and into the Cold War, many kinds of music were banned in Russia. Decadent Western songs, of course—jazz, mambo, rock and roll—but also Russian folk music, including songs from the gulags. Smuggling in LPs was dangerous, and though there were record lathes—German; spoils of war—vinyl, shellack, and lacquer were hard to buy unless you were producing recordings of Stalin's speeches. Then someone figured out discarded X-ray film could be used as a substitute. Trace a circle using a plate, cut it out with a pair of scissors, burn a hole into the middle with a cigarette. Onto images of broken wrists, rib cages, and skulls, bootleggers recorded songs by Ella Fitzgerald, W.C. Handy, Bill Haley & His Comets, Elvis.

My oncologist told me the CT scan showed a spot the size a BB on my lung and "flecks" on my liver. When I asked to see the scans, he looked surprised. "I'm not a radiologist," he said. "I just read the report." I pushed, and his PA told us we had to go to another exam room, one with a computer that could access the images. We followed her across the hall, and after much clicking, I saw my insides in gray and black. I'd expected something like an X-ray, a single picture of my torso taken as I lay supine, but a CT scan is a series of horizontal slices viewed as if the patient is standing and you're looking down from above. My lungs were black ovals that changed shape slightly in each slide. When he reached the point where the report noted the BB-sized spot, he looked for a second and said, "You probably had a bad cold when you were a kid." He clicked to the image of my liver that was supposed to show "flecks," squinted, took of his glasses, put his face near the screen, shook his head. "Do you see anything?" he asked me.

It's hard to tell if the murky image onto which "Heartbreak Hotel" is recorded is of a heart. I can see ribs and what look like veins. The original, released in January 1956, is two minutes and eight seconds long, the undated version on the X-ray one minute and fifty-four seconds. Fourteen seconds lost. The staticky bootleg begins and ends in medias res, almost like a door opens to a room where a forbidden record is playing—*it's down at the end of Lonely Street*—then closes before the tune ends: *Well, they're so lone—*

FOR MARCEL DUCHAMP & JOSEPH CORNELL

DC is where I learned nostalgia, city of museums and monuments, gigantic graveyard marked with memorials to the many, many dead.

Behind glass at the National Gallery, as if for sale (like everything everywhere), Duchamp's *Boîte-en-Valise,* his greatest hits made miniature: *Fountain, Nude Descending a Staircase, L.H.O.O.Q.,* etcetera. The first time I saw *Box in a Valise* I assumed he created a collection of tiny replicas between 1935 and 1940 because he saw coming a time when he'd need to travel light, his past distilled to fit inside a suitcase, his monuments small as memory. But the object label didn't mention Duchamp made twenty such collections, paid for by subscribers, and then in the decades following, 300 more in six additional editions. I've seen iterations in New York and Atlanta. The example in DC is not even one of the twenty he made in Paris before the German occupation. It's dated 1961.

Blocks and blocks of Shaw, the historically African American neighborhood, are no more than empty lots half-hidden by the false fronts of propped-up facades from old row houses and furniture stores. Developers have preserved quaint commercial signage and ornate keystones behind which cranes tall enough to build skyscrapers lift all day. During the riots after Dr. King was murdered, Shaw burned, was then rebuilt, and now it's again being razed. Vintage advertisements for Reagan-era go-go shows decorate the restaurant's gentrified exposed brick. I remember one night in the middle–'80s when *MEESE is a PIG* broadsides went up beside these same Trouble Funk and Experience Unlimited and Chuck Brown & The Soul Searchers posters.

The recently-renovated East Building of the National Gallery smells faintly of paint, as if what's hanging on the walls is still wet, all time collapsed to one day when all this stuff was new. This is where I used to come to meet my girlfriend after her Saturday shift at the information desk. We'd wander around for a little while and then enter the twilight as if it were normal one moment to be in the presence of art most people see only on postcards or in coffee-table books, if they see it at all, and the next to be walking toward the Metro station talking about friends or TV or where to get dinner. The triangular desk is still the same, the restrooms are still around the corner down by the gift shop where they used to be, but the payphones are gone. There's a staircase that feels like a secret because it's new to me, and it leads to the Duchamp. Across the small room there's a case with works by Joseph Cornell. Duchamp almost immediately became bored making Boîte-en-Valise over and over—Walter Benjamin surely has something to say about that—and in the early 1940s, while living in New York, he hired assistants to carry out the monotonous task of producing multiple tiny versions of his handful of masterpieces. One of those assistants was Joseph Cornell, who at time was just starting to make his own surrealist boxes. Discordant but logical connections—memories of that girlfriend and the smell of wet paint, Cornell working for Duchamp—amplify nostalgia.

My daughter's disappointed by the Metro's dingy Yellow Line trains, antiques I probably rode in high school, their carpets still stained and their crackling speakers still broadcasting mumbling conductors. dc space, where in 1989 I saw Fugazi, is now a Starbucks, and Chinatown, formerly gritty and wonderfully weird, has been cleaned up—there's a Chipotle and a Fudruckers and another Starbucks—but I tell my wife I'm sure this is the same dusty shop where nearly thirty years ago I bought a sandwich bag of warm fortune cookies, their warnings and promises about the future printed in mimeograph blue.

FOR THE ARTIST WHO DREW TWO PENISES

Beneath an eight o'clock evening sky blue and bright as noontime, a brace of bulbous cartoon cocks was chalked on the sidewalk beside the Commie Pool bus stop. The larger pointed west, the smaller east, toward Arthur's Seat. For a year I'd been worrying about not writing novels and I was trying to force my family trip to Scotland to inspire me. After seeing the graffiti by the bus stop, I came up with a vague idea about a middle-aged guy on a trip to Edinburgh writing apologies to all the women he felt he'd disappointed, including his wife, his daughter, and an ex whose biography was loosely based on the biography of a woman I'd dated in high school and college in the 1980s. When she was very young, that woman's family had fled Chile after Pinochet's police came looking for her lawyer father—and asked her where he was. But the idea was flat and forced: the guy was sorry for doing the kinds of things everyone should be sorry for doing if they did them, or the things he apologized for didn't warrant an apology; the apologies allowed / caused him to talk about sex, probably because of the chalked penises. This flat, forced idea made me feel like a failure when I thought about it, so I made myself not think about it. In a yard across the street from the small hotel where we were staying there grew a weird pine tree: spiky, spindly, tall, fragile, and out of place. One day my wife, my daughter, and I rode the bus to the botanic garden, and there I saw the same tree and learned what it was: *Monkey Puzzle (Araucaria araucana)*—native to Chile. Why fret about fiction when in Edinburgh the world gives me cocks drawn in chalk on the pavement outside the community swimming pool and the coincidence of thinking about Pinochet's police and twice encountering a tree native to the Andes?

FOR BASHŌ

In *Narrow Road to the Interior,* Bashō writes of visiting a thousand-year-old stone stela that records the building and repairing of Taga Castle: *Floods and landslides buried trails and markers, trees have grown and died, making this monument very difficult to find. The past remains hidden in clouds of memory. Still it returned to us memories from a thousand years before. Such a moment is the reason for a pilgrimage: infirmities forgotten, the ancients remembered, joyous tears trembled in my eyes.* That was 1689, and the tagajōi survives. Inscribed on it are the distances from the castle to the capital at Nara, the provinces of the Emishi, Kyoto, and the Ezo country. A text of dates and distances, beautiful because for more than thirteen hundred years it's presented an objective record—and because it wasn't intended to be beautiful. Late one June night, they removed from the town square of my Atlanta suburb the hundred-and-twelve-year-old obelisk that records the desires of Confederate losers to recast failure as victory, hatred as heritage. A couple of years before, someone sheathed the CSA memorial in rainbow macramé. The next day the yarn bomb was piled on the courthouse steps. I went inside and told the two Southern women at the little museum in the lobby they should collect the knitting, because it was part of history. They smiled and politely ignored me.

Later Bashō stands on a beach and *the summer rain-sky cleared to reveal a pale moon.* That happened here, too. I was walking the dogs through the subdivision. Bats hunted bugs above the warm pavement. A bottle rocket screamed. Dryer sheets perfumed the heavy air.

FOR CY TWOMBLY

A graffiti tag isn't meant to mimic the world it marks, nor to record anecdotal details of the tagger's life; instead, it's stylized text practiced and repeated. The trick is that each replicated tag looks unique—and spontaneous, scrawled, extemporaneous. A tag is simultaneously signature and alias. In first grade in Normal, Illinois, I learned how to move my pencil across paper to form a top-heavy J with its tail dangling below the line on which I then had to balance an O, a triangular S, and an H with a stem mirroring the J's tail. I wrote my name over and over; the goal was to make it look the same no matter how many times I wrote it. Cursive is the first thing I remember practicing. Recently I rode the 6 uptown to see Cy Twombly's *Dutch Interior* at the Met. In the City, every surface bears a mark, Holden Caulfield's post-war *fuck* long replaced by the cryptic language of taggers. Dutch Interior is a big painting, almost nine feet tall and ten feet wide, and Twombly's marks make it feel almost like a wall from the city outside: scribbles, smears, gobs of what looks like gum, a handprint, the string of numbers *1 2 3 4 5 6 7 8* repeated several times. And over what resembles a doodle of boobies, the word *detail* in lazy cursive my teacher would have scolded me for. The marks feel spontaneous, but of course they're not, of course that spontaneity is practiced, just like a tag, just like my name in cursive in first grade, just like the signature my surgeon Sharpie'd on my thigh, marking me as his, the last thing I remember happening before I went under. It was still there when I woke, tumor removed. Stasis mimicking action. Six weeks before, he'd drawn a doodle of a torso on a notepad and told me that in the old days they had to open up the abdomen to get to the colon—and he scribbled a jagged line from bellybutton to solar plexus to show me how. Then he doodled another torso and gave me the good news: progress meant that there now would only be four small incisions. Scale made those marks tiny. The ease of his doodles and scribbles and casual tick marks was practiced and precise. Happenstance? There is no happenstance.

FOR ANNA PAVLOVA

In the lot of the suburban Atlanta ballet studio, parents park, get out, and move to the passenger sides of our Camrys and minivans so our daughters can drive us home after Wednesday-night pointe class. We're nine months into the plague and I've got the windows down to let in mild December. *Everything sux,* my friend the poet texts me from Massachusetts. As if in response, from inside the building I'm parked beside my daughter texts me a video of herself rehearsing *The Dying Swan.* Her arms flutter. En pointe she glides across the room. She's lovely and graceful and perfect. She wears a surgical mask and Christmas pajama pants. When at the dance's end she's tucked into a tight shape, like a wounded bird, the ballet mistress says, "Don't fidget when you're dead."

FOR THE MASTER OF THE OSSERVANZA

Circa 1430/1450, The Master of the Osservanza, a member of the Sienese School, composes a continuous narrative painting of the meeting of Saint Antony of Egypt and Saint Paul the Anchorite. Centered at the bottom of the frame, Anthony embraces Paul, his journey through the desert to find the better hermit complete. Their heads are together, their gold-leaf haloes stacked. At their feet lie Anthony's two staffs. Anthony simultaneously appears in the middle of the painting—above, to the right, and smaller—halfway to Paul's hermitage. There Anthony encounters a centaur whom he asks for directions and who helpfully points the way. Anthony's beard and staff and the centaur's raised and bent fetlock are tipped at the same angle and cast no shadows. Anthony's gnarled staff (here he holds only one) mirrors the gnarled trunks of the trees of the forest though which he will pass to get to Paul. In the top left corner, the smallest Anthony commences his desert journey, one staff on his right shoulder, one in his left hand, flat halo like a sun bright against the trees behind him. He has had a dream in which he has seen Saint Paul is the superior hermit and is setting out to meet him. The eye is drawn first to the tallest version of Anthony at journey's end, then lead up the path he has traveled, through the twisted trees, to medium Anthony and the centaur who is perhaps a demon sent to scare him, perhaps a metaphor. Then the path falls off the edge of the painting's world for a moment before reappearing and heading behind a hill—and there is the smallest Anthony, up at the top, starting his pilgrimage beneath a halo-golden sky. His journey appears entire and concurrent.

For many years *The Meeting of Saint Anthony and Saint Paul* delighted me because the way time works in the painting mimics the way time works in memory: at once chronological and simultaneous. Things happen in sequence but also all at once. Outside of memory, time moves forward. We look forward to tomorrow and it dutifully arrives. Then one tomorrow a pandemic arrives—arrived. When we went into quarantine, the collapsed-yet-sequenced nature of time in *The Meeting of Saint Anthony and Saint Paul* became the way all time worked, inside and outside of memory. Days, weeks, months collapsed upon themselves and took place all at once along the twisting path on which Anthony is tempted and tested; confusing beasts spoke to me via Zoom and I tried my best to direct them and to follow their directions; every day was the same, no matter how it was different. Now I'm vaccinated and I travel Publix's terrazzo trails on my way to self-checkout the way Anthony made his way through the desert, past shelves once again filled with temptations—toilet paper and Lysol wipes and jugs of milk—but I can't seem to manage to separate memory-time from real-time. Cashiers and assistant managers tell me to have a nice day and I repeat the directive back at them. I wake up worried, no matter how many or few tasks are penciled into my datebook, and I keep worrying about those tasks until I fall asleep—and then I wake up worried, at the path's beginning again, always.

FOR GEORG CHRISTOPH LICHTENBERG

On the day in sunny September when I read in Lichtenberg, *As the few adepts in such things well know, universal morality is to be found in little everyday penny-events just as much as in great ones,* there's a sign at the Circle K alerting customers of a nationwide coin shortage, but instead of suggesting we reintroduce into circulation our hoarded nickels and dimes, it asks that we no longer pay in cash. One of the many things the never-ending pandemic makes me miss is coins, the slow counting out, the hand-to-hand transfer. When I was a kid, I rolled pennies in brown paper sleeves, a lot of effort to get two quarters and a Dum-Dums lollypop from the grinning bank tellers, but I had all the time in the world. In the late 1980s, when I was a student at the University of Maryland, I fed quarters into a coin-op IBM Selectric. Twenty-five cents bought fifteen minutes of typing time. I read *Waiting for Godot* waiting on an orange couch outside that room filled with typewriters in the basement of Hornbake Library. I remember the disproportionate heartbreak caused by a coin, Canadian or in some other way unacceptable, rattling repeatedly into the payphone's return when I didn't have another in my pocket to replace it, and therefore couldn't afford the minutes to complete my call. When she was not yet ten, my daughter and I spent an afternoon sorting a jar of pennies before taking it to the CoinStar machine at the grocery store—long gone are the days of paper rolls and Dum-Dums—and to our delight we found one minted in the 1890s. It went into a Ziploc bag she labeled *Old Pennie! Do*

Not Touch!! Years later, in Chicago to look at colleges, walking through Lincoln Park, I said to her "You can tell a lot about a neighborhood by the plentitude or paucity of pennies on the pavement near its bus stops."

FOR E.M. CIORAN

In carpool line I read *Write books only if you are going to say in them the things you would never dare confide in anyone* and I think "Yes, Cioran, yes." The trouble with *The Trouble With Being Born* is that after almost every aphorism I think "Yes, Cioran, yes." I pencil checkmark after checkmark into the margins while waiting for my daughter. But this isn't usually why I read books. I want to disagree too. But Cioran makes me *like to read the way a chorus girl does: identifying myself with the author and the book. Any other attitude makes me think of dissecting corpses.* I've got the windows down. Somewhere behind me an idling SUV's AC cycles even though it's barely seventy and there's a breeze. *Once we reject lyricism, to blacken the page becomes an ordeal: what's the use of writing in order to say exactly what we had to say?* When I look up, the reflection of a jet plane high above crosses the back window of the Prius in front of me. *When we are young, we take a certain pleasure in our infirmities. They seem so new, so rich! With age, they no longer surprise us, we know them too well. Now, without anything unexpected in them, they do not deserve to be endured.* I take a picture of a page, edit Richard Howard's translation down to a single line, and text the excerpt to the friend who introduced me to the book: *I would give the whole universe and all of Shakespeare for a grain of ataraxy.*

FOR VIKTOR SHKLOVSKY

I didn't stop to take the snapshot and now I can't: the gas station's mansard roof has been peeled off as part of a renovation and gone are the letters, painted over in the same yellow the roof was painted, spelling out *RESTAURANT*. Once the letters had been red, maybe blue, maybe green, and I'd never noticed them, their normalcy making them invisible, but when the roof and the sign were sprayed the same primary color last year, suddenly the letters drew my eye every time I drove past. Everywhere we are witnessing the disappearance of the shitty—the pay phone with its receiver torn off vanishes one day from the Chinese restaurant's parking lot, the hand-lettered sign in the window of the tailor's is replaced with a generic placard, the Quonset hut where they fixed old Mustangs is razed to make way for the mixed-use development. Losing worn things makes them dear, no matter how tattered and useless they've become. In thrift stores I sort through piles of 45s. Not too long ago I came across a stack pulled from a jukebox in 1986: Madonna, Pet Shop Boys, David Lee Roth. I was seventeen that summer, the summer between high school and college. Almost four decades later I stood in Last Chance fondling the past and heard again those songs playing in my memory.

FOR ANTONIO BIGGI

In Rome in June 2001, I took the Metro to Piramide, where I was surprised to find, down a dim hallway on the way to the toilets, a faded mural celebrating Mussolini. After I left the station, I walked around the Pyramid of Cestius, built a dozen years before the birth of Christ, to get to the Protestant Cemetery, where I read *Here lies One / Whose Name was writ in Water* on Keats' stone and saw the slab under which lie Shelley's ashes—but for more than two decades I couldn't get out of my mind the image of that colorful mural. I returned to Rome and to the Piramide station in June 2023 and I found memory had betrayed me: there isn't a fascist mural; rather, there's a fascist bas-relief. And the sculpture celebrating man's three roles—solider on top, father in the middle, laborer at the bottom—isn't down the hallway to the men's room, but by the door opening onto that hallway. Orange plastic construction fencing, ubiquitous in Rome, on which hangs a small sign reading *DIVIETO DI ACCESSO*, leans against the bottom third—appropriately the part of the sculpture that shows laborers at work with pick, shovel, and jackhammer. In a city filled with museums and archeological sites and graveyards, all exhaustively labeled with explanatory signage in multiple languages, it's weird to come upon a sculpture lacking a note identifying artist and artwork. The bas-relief is dingy and dinged up, much like the station entrance, white stone grayed by the city's ancient grit. The noses and cheeks of the men, women, and children are the dirtiest parts. The internet tells me

Piramide opened in 1955, and that the sculpture was made in 1938 by Antonio Biggi, an artist who in the late 1930s and early 1940s regularly exhibited his work at the Sindacale Fascista del Lazio and who after the war won a contest to design the bronze doors of Saint Peter's Basilica. The internet doesn't explain how a pre-World War II Fascist bas-relief ended up in a post-war subway station in Rome. So is this about memory? Is the orange safety fence and the lack of an object label a metaphor for the way memory processes Biggi's homage to blood and soil: as the years pass, it falls slowly into disrepair and anonymity? And what does it mean that, even after standing in front of the carved stone in the dim vestibule, I still remember the faded colors of the mural, the reds and blues and yellows, impossibly illuminated by summer sunlight?

NOTES

For Theodor Adorno

Adorno, Theodor. *Minima Moralia: Reflections from Damaged Life*. London & New York: Verso, 2020

For Susan Sontag

Sontag, Susan. *On Photography*. New York: Dell, 1979

For Roland Barthes

Barthes, Roland. *Camera Lucida*. New York: Hill & Wang, 1987

For Jonathan Swift and Claude Monet

Swift, Jonathan. *Selected Prose Works of Jonathan Swift*. London: The Cresset Press, 1949

For Borges

Borges, Jorge Luis. *Labyrinths*. New York: New Directions, 1964.

For Bashō

Bashō, Matsuo. *Narrow Road to the Interior and Other Writings*. Boston & London: Shambhala, 2000

For Georg Christoph Lichtenberg

Lichtenberg, Georg Christoph. *The Waste Books*. New York: New York Review Books, 2000

For E.M. Cioran

Cioran, E.M. *The Trouble with Being Born.* New York: Arcade Publishing, 2012

ACKNOWLEDGMENTS

This book wouldn't exist without the artists who inspire me, including those I gloss in these commonplaces, especially Lola Russell and Kathryn Pratt Russell.

Many thanks to the editors who gave these essays their attention and support:

J. Robert Lennon, *Epoch:* "For Theodor Adorno," "For Susan Sontag," "For Cy Twombly," "For Antonio Biggi"; *Electric Literature:* "For Kathryn," "For Borges"

Daniel Schonning & Geoffrey Babbitt, *Seneca Review:* "For Anna Pavlova"

Frederick Bartheleme, *New World Writing Quarterly:* "For Dexys Midnight Runners," "For Robert F. Simon," "For Fugazi," "For DJ Scott LaRock & Jasper Johns," "For Roland Barthes," "For Elvis"

Carl Annarummo, *Greying Ghost Pamphlet Sounds:* "For Madonna"

Lynn Mundell, *Centaur:* "For Georg Christoph Lichtenberg"

Elizabeth Foulke, *Ocean State Review:* "For Marcel Duchamp & Joseph Cornell"

Michael Mejia, *Western Humanities Review:* "For Henry James," "For Jonathan Swift & Claude Monet," "For Jean-Michel Basquiat," "For Bashō"

Christopher Merkner & Jennifer S. Davis, *Copper Nickel:* "For Joseph Cornell & Edward Hopper"

Nellie Papsdorf, *Sonora Review:* "For Viktor Shklovsky"

JOSH RUSSELL's story collection is *King of the Animals*, and his novels are *Yellow Jack*, *My Bright Midnight*, and *A True History of the Captivation, Transport to Strange Lands & Deliverance of Hannah Guttentag*. He's Distinguished University Professor and Director of the Creative Writing Program at Georgia State University, and he lives in Decatur, Georgia.

❊

COLOPHON

Text is set in a digital version of Jenson, designed by Robert Slimbach in 1996, and based on the work of punchcutter, printer, and publisher Nicolas Jenson. The titles here are not in Futura, as is our custom, since Futura is certainly the best font for titles, but in Neue Kabel for mimesis.

www.ingramcontent.com/pod-product-compliance
Lightning Source LLC
LaVergne TN
LVHW051021080826
845145LV00009B/2730

* 9 7 8 1 9 7 1 7 4 0 0 0 3 *